A Lone Survivor

A Lone Survivor

Frances Armbrust

To order additional copies of this book, contact:
Xlibris Corporation
1-888-795-4274
www.Xlibris.com
Orders@Xlibris.com
36858

DEDICATION

I would like to dedicate this book to Jerry Jones whom I have known for many years. We have had a good relationship; we enjoy arguing Jerry has been a good dispatcher and: a long time friend of mine. I made money while driving under her. Now that I am retired: I like to talk to her in the evening as she does her work. She has had a hard time since her husband's death: May God bless her the rest of her years.

THE ART ON THE BOOK COVER WAS DOWN BY AN UNKNOWN CAB DRIVER-FIFTY-EIGHT YEARS AGO FOR BEST CABS INC.; HE HAS SINCE PASSEDAWAY. NO ONE SEEMS TO BE ABLE TO REMEMBER HIS NAME.

THE SKATCHES IN THE BOOK; WAS DONE BY VALLERIE CAMBEL MY DAUGHTER.

THE STORY IS ABOUT AN OLD CAB DRIVER WHO NEVERED MARRIED AFTER HE LOST HIS GIRL IN A CAR ACCIDENT WHILE IN KOREA.

INTRODUCTION

This is the story of John Hooker as told to me by him. He said, "I have had many experience's in my life, I have always tried to be an honest man, and remember the teaching of my parents. I have never been in jail, and hope I never will be.

I had one love that I lost in a car accident while serving my country in Korea. My parents died three days apart this was a bad time for me.

I am a loner and have been most of my life, don't get me wrong; I may be a loner but, I am a survivor. I am a 74-year-old virgin male and proud to be one. I have found it necessary to pull myself up by the bootstraps a few times after I hit rock bottom. I have slept many a night on a park bench after my parents died, and there was no one to care who I was or where I had to sleep. I lived off of $112.00 for many years during this time I learned the meaning of being hungry. I have had one drink of alcohol one time in my life, it made me very sick and I never touched the stuff after that. You don't have to be a drunk to be homeless.

I enjoy hanging out at the Cab Company and visiting with all my old pals. There is really not to many of them left these days. Most of them have passed away but, there is still a few people of my generation left."

I have lived a long life: maybe I can live another twenty years. I am looking forward to my reunion with Molly and my parents when the time comes. Until then I will enjoy the large family of the cab company and the cab drivers. I miss working, but my large adopted family keeps me from being lonely for the first time since I lost my Molly and my parents I feel a part of something and someone. I will never go hungry or sleep on another park bench or feel the pain of hungry again. Someone cares about me again. This is a good feeling. I almost forgot what it felt like to be wanted, needed and cared for.

CHAPTER ONE

When my parents were married, my mother's father and mother weren't too happy about it; they didn't like my father at all. Mother's parents wanted her to marry a man with more material possessions and education. After a while they realized that Mother was happy and content with her lot in life; much more so than her sisters, who had married into wealth. For many years my mother's side of the family shunned my father. They never did like my father, but finally they accepted the fact that he was part of the family. I may have had something to do with that when I was born. My grandmother on my mother's side of the family loved me with all her heart. This meant even though they didn't like Father they had to accept him because of me.

Two of my aunts never married the other sisters constantly criticized them for not marrying and having a family. My grandparents weren't too happy with the her children that was doing the criticizing she felt it was none of their business.

I was born during the depression on March 12th, 1933. My Parents were great and wonderful people; I loved them very much. My father worked as a hired hand on a farm. We lived in a house on a four-acre plot. Our house had no indoor plumbing. We had an outhouse in the back of our house far enough away so we couldn't smell it. We owned a few chicken and pigs for meat and eggs. The farmer who owned the property let us grow a garden and have our own stock. Mother always raised the best garden for miles around. This was a wonderful place to grow up. I was very happy has a child.

We had a neighbor that was a butcher; he butchered our pigs for us as a favor to my parents once a year. When he needed vegetables mother gave them to him from her garden as a favor this was kind of a trade off deal. He butchered our pigs in return mother gave him produce from her garden in the summer. My mother canned enough food from her garden so there would be enough for both families with some to spare for the needy people when things got too hard for them. There were a lot of people that lost their homes, they had no money to pay a doctor or no food to put in their stomach my parents helped people as much as it was possible. This was okay with the farmer that owned the property too. People cared and looked after each other most of the time, in those days.

As soon as I was old enough to learn the difference between plants and weeds it was my job to help mother hoe the four-acre garden. My mother had what was known as a green thumb. We had plenty to eat from our garden but she needed help, being the only child; I was it. I got stuck with feeding the chickens and pigs as well. Which I truly resented doing. As I got older I had to clean out the chicken house. In those days a child had to work the same as an adult to keep food in their bellies. I learned to enjoy my chores after a while. I found it fascinating to watch the little seeds grow into larger plants and wondered how it was possible for this to happen.

My mother did all the housework, and made most of the clothes we wore by hand. Mother washed our clothes on a scrub board in tubs out in the yard in the summer. In the winter she scrubbed them, in the living room and tried not to make a big mess. Winter and summer she hung our clothes on a clothesline in the backyard. I remember how red her hands looked in the winter after she had hung our clothes outside. Mother ironed our clothes with what was called a flat iron; it was made out of pure iron and very heavy. She had to heat them on top of the stove. It seemed that mother was always; always smiling. She seemed to enjoy her chores.

When I started school we moved closer to town-to-town where my father took on a couple of additional jobs a blacksmith and welder. My father also worked for the Wichita Eagle Beacon in the circulation department. He recruited paperboys. My mother didn't work outside of the house she had enough to do to keep the family in food and clothes. Even in when we moved closer town my mother had a large garden that I maintained for her. She always grew and canned enough vegetables to help her neighbors and people in need. I found it hard to adjust to life in our new home and I noticed that Mother didn't seem to smile as she used to Mother didn't like living so close to town she wasn't a town person.—She just never felt at ease and neither did I?

I started delivering papers when I was about seven years old. This was a very hard job for a child as young as I was. Sometimes I got so tired I wondered if I could finish my route on time to do my chores plus do the hoeing and weeding in the garden. I was the youngest child with paper routes to throw in the territory. I was quite proud of this while it lasted.

When I was about nine I took a day off from delivering papers and asked a friend to do my route. Grandfather smuggled me on the train. He was born in 1833 and died in 1945 he worked for the Santa Fe as an engineer all his life. He had a fireman that could throw forty pounds of coal in each hand one right after the other into the boiler. One day he smuggled me on the train, he was running late. We came to a long stretch of straight track about fifty miles long grandfather opened up that engine and we were going one-hundred forty miles an hour down that track to make up time. Boy was I ever scared! don't get me wrong I loved the train ride but the speed grandfather went scared me to death. We made our destination on time. I believe no one else could have done this but my grandfather. I truly enjoyed being with him looked up to him; he was my idol and mentor at the time.

When grandfather retired in 1943 he was 110 years old; but not ready to give up the Santa Fe just yet. He bought a Steam Engine from the company. He placed it in his back yard for old time's sake. The engine was one hundred thirty feet long. The drive wheels that provided the power for the engine was fourteen feet high. He wanted that engine as a memorial to his life. Our neighbor next door hated that engine and he picked no bones about it. He argued all the time with my grandfather over that engine he even went to the city and complained. But my grandfather had a permit for it and there was nothing our neighbor could do. The engine was legally my grandfather's. My grandfather died two years later in 1945 at the ripe old age of 112 years old when he was hit by a garbage truck. The world lost a wonderful man when ;Grandfather was hit by that truck. My mother took it very hard. My Grandmother on my mother's side died a few years later.

One day we went to visit one of my friends, when we returned the engine was gone. We suspected our neighbor got rid of it but he would never admit to it. The pride and joy of my grandfather's life was gone forever. I missed that old train engine more than any one knew. I guess I loved it as much as my grandfather did. When the engine was sitting in the yard I felt grandfather was still with us, after it was gone my grandfather was gone too. When the engine was gone I finally accepted the fact that grandfather was gone forever.

My Grandmother and Grandfather had 15 children as their children grew up, married and had children of their own. They all treated each other like a great big family. Each one looked after the other ones needs. I was an only child and spoiled rotten. I got my way pretty much and didn't have a lot of time to be lonely; I had plenty of friends and family to hang out with. Many times the whole family had supper together. We had a good time. We helped each other with our chores and farm work when some one needed help. We did not argue and fight between ourselves. We shared what we had with one another without complaint. I guess that's just the way it was in those days. That's what made life so great back then.

One Saturday a strong storm came through our area, Sunday morning it was still very windy with strong gust of wind at times. I was about ten years old. Our preacher was a big man he weighed about three hundred pounds. Dressed in a white suit as the preacher approached the pulpit he said, "Before we get started I have an announcement I need to make, I have a problem and may have to run to the outhouse without any notice. I beg for your forgiveness for this and thank you for your patience. If this happens Carol can lead you in a song or if you wish you can just visit with one another I'm sure we don't do enough of that with all your busy schedules this will give you the chance to make up for lost time, so take advantage of the opportunity if it comes."

Our preacher began his sermon he got into it pretty good and suddenly he made a beeline to the outhouse. As he ran across the wood floors of the Church he sounded like an elephant running across the floor. All the children started laughing at how funny it was to watch a three hundred pound man running in Church. A child jumped up from his seat and said, "We're not supposed to run in Church we get spanked for running in Church." His mother quickly tried to silence him without success. The child went on to say, "He sounds like a fat horse running on a wooden porch and he looks funny." This child mocked him running along behind the preacher until his mother was able to collar him. His mother shamed him verbally in front of everyone.

The congregation decided to get caught up on the town gossip while the preacher was out. Suddenly we heard the preacher yelling and even cursing if you can belief that? The whole congregation ran out side to see what the problem was. We found the outhouse had blown over by a gust of wind our preacher had fallen in the hole designed to hold the waste. This hole was at least waist deep on the preacher; with human waste. The hole itself was about shoulder high on the preacher. The outhouse was turned over on top of the hole.

After a few minutes a couple of the brothers in the congregation turned the outhouse over, and pulled our preacher out of the hole used as a holding tank for the outhouse, which the outhouse set on top of. The preacher was pulled from the hole, with his pants around his ankles covered with poop. Poop was still running out of his behind. His white suite was not white any more. We had a very embarrassed Preacher that Sunday, needless to say church was over. People went home thank-full that the Preacher had not been hurt, but laughing about his predicament, which really wasn't very funny for him. As the people were leaving the scene the little bratty child that had spoken up before said, "That's what he gets for running in the Church. God got even with him good, and I bet he never runs in a Church again. I know I will never run in the Church again I don't want to make God mad at me."

Our poor preacher found another flock to supervise; because he could not stand the embarrassment of what had happened to him in the outhouse. We received a brand new preacher that was new to us and that didn't know our ways. My nephew and I initiated our new preacher with my aunt's dandelion wine.

My Aunt had a wine-still out in the woods away from the house; where she made dandelion wine. Dandelion wine; has no taste and no color it looks like water, but it sure has quite a punch to it; it is strong stuff. In the summer my Aunt always kept a pitcher of dandelion wine with ice in it on the table in the living room for this was usually visitor's day.

That Saturday our new preacher paid my aunt a visit. My aunt had some chores she needed to do so she went about her chores before visiting with the preacher. A cold pitcher of dandelion wine with a glass was setting in the middle of the table the preacher thought it was water. He poured himself a ten ounce glass of what he believed was cold water, and then he poured himself another glassful, then another half glass. My nephew and I were standing back just watching him we knew what he was drinking but, we said nothing and thought it was funny.

When my Aunt came back from her chores the preacher tried to stand up as gentlemen did in those days when a lady walked into the room. The preacher stepped forward and fell face down in the living room floor he had passed out from the dandelion wine. My Aunt was a big strong woman, my nephew and I was about twelve years of age we tried to put the preacher on the couch he was just too heavy for us to handle. He was so relaxed it was like trying to pick up a two hundred pound rag doll. We had to wait until my Uncle came home to get him laid out on the couch, which was not for several hours yet. My Uncle came home and we managed to get him laid on the couch. He slept for seven hours before he opened his eyes. The four of us managed to get him in the old truck so my Uncle and I could take him home he still was so drunk he couldn't walk without help. When we got him to his house we needed help to get him out of the truck. I have never seen a woman throw such a fit in my life especially a preacher's wife she had never seen her husband drunk before and BOY! Was she ever mad! She was still preaching hell and damnation to him when we left. My uncle and I laughed all the way home.

The poor preacher was passed out drunk on his couch from what he thought was water; he didn't hear a word of his wife's preaching. Needless to say our preacher was unable to deliver his sermon the next morning. My nephew and I should have stopped him from drinking the wine but we thought it would be funny to see a preacher drunk. I am sure he didn't think it was so funny when his wife got through with him the next morning.

The next time our preacher seen my Aunt he said, "Ruthie your water sure carries quite a punch I don't understand what happened to me the last time I was here all I did is drink a pitcher of cold water. The preacher was never told it was not water that he drank. I have laughed about that through out the years.

When I was about twelve years old my nephew and I went to visit Aunt Ruthie on my mother's side of the family. My Uncle owned a one thousand acre farm. My Aunt raised three thousand chickens. She was one of the first people that raised chicken without them ever touching the ground. Her chicken house was 200-yard wide and 500 yards long. Inside the chicken house there was wire cubicles with a wire bottom in them under the cubicles there was rubber like crates with wheels on them that caught the chicken poop. We were quite unhappy when my Aunt asks us to clean out the rubber crates in the chicken house. That is the last thing a twelve-year-old boy wants to do. I had to do this many times after that to my regret.

When we went into the chicken house at first we were astonished by what we saw. Our mouths dropped clear down to our knees it seemed. Then we laughed until we couldn't laugh any more. All the chickens were wearing dresses and bonnets. When we finally got control of our laughter and finished emptying the rubber crates. We asked my Aunt about the chickens wearing dresses and bonnets she said, "I made the dresses and bonnets for them don't you think they are cute? Everything has to have its hour of fame this is their hour of fame, for they are going to market next week." I asked her how she kept the clothes on the chickens. She said, "Where there is a will, there is a way. It wasn't easy getting them on, but keeping them on. is simple." Then she walked away from us telling us supper was ready. One week later the whole three thousand chickens went to market my aunt started all over again with her chickens. We felt like she was weird however we didn't dare say that out loud, we would have got our butts fanned.

I delivered papers for several years until I was fifteen. I learned a lot about human nature when I was delivering papers especially while trying to collect my money for the papers I delivered to people. The worst part of this job was collecting. Many times the people didn't have the money to pay for their paper sometimes they could only pay part of it. Other times they just wouldn't even open the door. Sometimes people seen me coming and went out the back door. If a boy did not collect all the money owed to the Wichita

Beacon he had to pay the difference out of his pocket so I went back to these people's house that did not pay many times, trying to get paid for my work. To many times I had to eat the cost of a customer's bill.

One time in particular I remember my paper bill was forty dollars. I could only collect thirty six of it I had to pay the four dollars out of my pocket that week instead of earning money from my paper route it cost me money. I remember a paper customer of mine Mr. Mould that owed me forty cents I was fourteen years old at the time. Thirty years later I ran into Mr. Mould and he paid me my forty cents. People use to say he was so tight that he would squeeze the tits off a pig if he could. Believe me he tried to squeeze blood out of a turnip many times.

Delivering papers didn't excuse me from my outdoor chores they had to be done too. I worked hard as a child but never in my life have I been hungry. My parents were very independent people and taught me to be independent as well. We never ask anyone for anything or complained about how hard our life was. My parents were always willing to help a neighbor in need when and if they needed help. I learned a lot of very valuable lessons from my parents at an early age. I have lived by these values all my life and I thank God from the bottom of my heart my parents loved me enough to teach these lesson to me these lessons have helped me survive many times.

When I turned 15 a friend of my father's who was a custom wheat cutter invited me to come along and help him in the wheat harvest. My father delivered my papers for me while I worked in the wheat harvest. We harvested wheat from South Texas all the way to Canada; I learned how to be a good and trustworthy helper in the wheat fields. When I was seventeen I was taught how to operate a combine this was long before combines had air conditioning. I became the main combine operator before I was eighteen. I worked in the summer and saved my money to pay for my schooling in the winter. Each year I had some spending money left to buy clothes and even have a little fun with after I learned not to give all my money to my friends.

The first summer when I returned with money I suddenly had a lot of friends, or should I say my money did. To my sorrow I learned when I wasted or gave away my money I did without the necessities of life this helped me to grow up faster. My parents let me learn the hard way how to spend my money and figure out who really were my friends it really didn't take me long to learn these lessons.

When I came back from the wheat harvest my father said, "If you want something you have to figure out a way to get it. First think about how much you want it and how hard you want to work for it. No one is just going to hand you what you want. If you want something bad enough you will be willing to go after it no mater what it takes. Or you will never achieve your goals. "I remembered that statement my father made to me all my life. When I want something no job is too menial for me to do as long as it is an honest job. I have done many jobs other people stuck their nose up at but I felt proud of myself because I have never intentionally done something I thought was dishonest. My father always followed this motto and was satisfied with his life.

It was hot working in the wheat harvest the only thing we had between us and the sun was an umbrella. We worked long hours and were so tired at the end of the day we didn't feel like playing around we went straight to bed. I enjoyed working the wheat harvest I enjoyed being busy. I became very close to my fathers friend. But soon his son took over the family business and I was not too fond of him. It was impossible for me to get along with

When I was about 15 I had just returned from working the harvest, a friend of mine ask to borrow $10. I gave it to him and went on home. Late in the evening the sheriff knocked on our door. I answered the door and told him my father wasn't home.

The sheriff said, "I didn't come to see your father, I came to see where were you between eight and midnight."

I said, "I was at home" and my mother verified this.

The sheriff said, "Did you give James any money?"

I said, "Yes."

The sheriff said," James gave Ben $5. to get him a bottle of whiskey last night, he got drunk, and beat the shit out of Ben. Now James is sitting in my jail. I wonder if you know anything about this?"

My mother said "John was at home by 8:30 last night."

The sheriff said, "Okay, goodnight" and left. James was no longer my friend. My father wouldn't let me associate with him anymore. He raised cane anytime he thought I had seen James.

In my senior year of high school I met the love of my life her name was Molly. She was the most beautiful girl I have ever seen, I loved her with all my heart and soul she felt the same way about me. I felt I just had to have her as my wife. She worked in a bank as a teller after school on Saturday. I was so proud of her achievement, she was indeed special to me in every way. I am unable to explain the feeling of love I felt for her and that I knew she felt for me. I was floating on cloud nine at this time. The world couldn't have been better to me. We spent as much time together as was possible, which was not nearly enough to satisfy us.

I started thinking about joining the Marines. This was a big decision for me because Wichita was an Army town. A few of my buddies and I were the odd balls we wanted to join the Marines. I took a lot of flack from my friends because I wanted to join the Marines instead of the Army. All my friends that had joined the Army acted like they thought they were hot stuff. They thought their manure didn't stink. I didn't even like them any more because I knew what they really were; none of them was hot stuff as they pretended to be. That is what made me want to join the Marines and not the Army. When I was asked why I was joining the Marines I simple said, "Because I want to," I knew I had to serve my country so I felt I may as well do it the way I wanted to. I was proud to be different then the people who had once been my friends. I didn't want to be the show off that they were. I didn't want to stoop down to their level I felt I was better then that. I was to busy for that kind of crap. When I wasn't with Molly I was with a friend.

There were three of us boys that hang out together. We had known each other most of our life where one was the other two could be found. We got into a little trouble we didn't do any breaking and entering or destroy any body's property. We never got into trouble with the law almost, but we were lucky the police in our town were friends of ours they also knew our parents and knew they would bring us back into line when they learned we had done something wrong. Just the same we found plenty of mischief to get into we were by far not angels. I was a little bit wild in those days but I did nothing really seriously wrong just got into a lot of mischief that annoyed people. And made myself look like a fool at times. If one of us had money we shared it with each other's, we were like brothers for a long time.

Larry's father owned a junkyard he was allowed to drive any car in the junkyard as long as he didn't take it off the property. Many times the three of us boys would take one of the cars for a joy ride without permission. None of us had a driver license we didn't even think about getting one because we were farmers and farm children were allowed to run errands for their parents in those days without having to worry about the law even when we were 18 years of age we didn't worry about getting a drivers license.

We started sneaking cars out of the junkyard at about15 years of age and had never been caught at it until now. Larry's father had acquired an old hearse from the town funeral home. I myself never drove the cars Larry did the driving because his father was the owner of the junkyard. We decided it would be fun to take the old hearse for a joyride this time. So brave, as old get out, we took the hearse at about five or six PM after his father had closed the business for the night. We drove through the counties without any lights hoping not to be seen. At about midnight we started to cross a bridge and noticed that the Deputy Sheriff was sitting on the other side of the bridge we quickly turned the hearse around and headed the other way. But who and behold he had spotted us and the chass was on. He chased us for a while before we decided to pull over. This is one time it paid for our parents to be friends with the Deputy Sheriff.

He bawled us out pretty good, and said, "Take the hearse back, and don't tell anyone that you took it or that I knew anything about it." He was very stern, he let us know he should arrest us, and he would if we didn't do as we were told. We felt lucky; we could have gone to jail.

We immediately took the hearse back to the junkyard. We thought we had got away with our great adventure but it was just the beginning. Even though we were 18 to our surprise our parents were waiting for us when we got home and they were very upset. The Deputy Sheriff had paid them a visit this was not a pleasant night for any of us. We knew we deserved whatever punishment our parents decided to give to us. We had been sneaking cars out of the junkyard for at least three years now and never been caught. Of course we didn't tell our parents that, we just took what we knew we had coming and didn't protest. We quietly listened to our parent's as they chewed our butts out which they definitely did a good job of.

The next day I said good-by to my darling sweetheart. I left for boot camp to learn how to defend our country. I stood tall held my chin up, I felt proud of myself, and I felt important.

I was off to Boot Camp in San Diego which I managed to survive it was hard for me in Boot Camp even though I was a strong healthy young man and had worked hard as a child. Up until now I knew my job and did my jobs willingly. In Boot Camp it was different the sergeants didn't speak to me like I was a human. They yelled their orders at the top of their lungs I was no dummy I could do as I was told without them yelling at me. I was a farm boy but I was not stupid I resented the sergeant's attitude toward the privates. Don't get me wrong I believe the citizens of our country should stand up and do our part to keep our people safe and protect our country. I just think it is wrong to talk to people like my sergeant talked to us.

The boots we had to ware were not much to look at, but they were comfortable and protected our feet and lower legs from any snakes or other critters, for that I was thankful. The food wasn't as bad as the rumors I had heard. In fact I liked it very well.

Finally Boot Camp was over, I went home for a week. Molly and I decided it was better for me to serve our country before we were married. It would be too hard for us to be separated for four years after having spent only a few days together as man and wife. So I said good-by to my high school sweetheart not realizing it would be the last time I would ever see her. If I had it to do over again I would have married her before I went to boot camp. To have a few days with her would have been better for me; then me never knowing what it was like to make love to my precious Molly. At least I would have had some memories to hold on to. Not marrying Molly was the biggest mistake I have ever made. But hindsight is always better then foresight this is one mistake I will never forgive myself for making I had put my country before my Molly I thought we were doing what was best for our eventual marriage. What a fool I was! Not to marry her while I had the chance. She had promised to wait for me, I didn't even think about the possibility that she wouldn't be or that something could happen that she had no control over.

In 1953 I entered the Marines where I spent the next 8 years of my life. I saw many things in Korea that I can't bring myself to talk about. I can tell you life in the Marines was not easy in those days. It was hard to accept some of the things that I saw. Some things made me sick at the stomach and frightened me to death. I couldn't show my fear; I would've been considered less than a man if I had. I was too proud to let anyone see how frightened I was; I had to prove that I was a man. I learned to accept the harsh words of our commanders and realize they were only doing what was necessary to teach us how to survive in a hot battle.

John Hooker in Marine uniform.

CHAPTER TWO

I was sent to Korea in a combat unit of 36 men we were constantly under fire. Four months later there were only 12 of us left, the rest had been killed. We were on a hill surrounded by our enemies it seemed the more we killed the more our enemies multiplied. Our Countries Troops couldn't help us if they tried to bomb the enemy from the air, they would have killed us too. They couldn't get to us by ground surrounded us. We were on our own there was no way anyone could help us at this time. That day had been on duty about eight hours. It was very cold about 10 degrees we were freezing our buns off and wonder if we would make it through the day.

The ground was rock we were on the side of a mountain going up a trail when we were ambushed. There seemed to be no place we could shield ourselves from the enemies relentless on coming bullets. One of my comrades spotted some large rocks about 15 feet high we ran toward them. There were a bunch of rocks grouped together some of the rocks had openings in them so we could crawl between them. But we had to find the boulders that had openings while we were under enemy fire. One of my comrades and I jumped between one of the sets of rocks another Marine my close friend, crawled into another group of rocks. We could see Ben Able across from us, our comrade Able that was alone in a group of rocks soon learned he was not alone he had company. Ben Able said, "Something is moving and it's not me, it's moving under my butt." Suddenly he started screaming Help me! Help me!

I was only about four feet away I could see a snake crawling out from between his legs. We told him not to move to stand as still as he could. We were unable to get to him because of the flying bullets, so he tried to run to our group of rocks. In the process the enemy fire mowed him down he was killed. The noise from the firing or the fact that the snakes had company made 100's of snakes crawl from the group of rocks where he was hiding. My other comrade and I were lucky—the snakes didn't like us, or maybe they were only trying to get away from their unwanted intruder. Hundreds of snakes crawled up the mountain and didn't bother us. By the time we were relieved there were only five of us left. The rest were dead bodies lying all around us, mowed down by the enemy's fire.

The base was about 5 miles way from the area we were patrolling, supposed to be in a safe area; the truth being there was no safe area. While we were under enemy fire, the Marines who had the detail of bringing us food couldn't get to us. A few times we did without food for several days until it was safe for someone to bring the food to us. The rocks were even colder at night; sometimes I was sure we would freeze to death before morning if a bullet didn't get us first.

While I was in Korea during the above combating my beloved wife to be was killed in a car accident it was no ones fault it just happened. Of course I didn't learn about it right away. I was on the front lines and it was hard for the military to get mail to us. When I finally I learned about my beautiful Molly's death I just fell to pieces, I lost it. I no longer cared weather I lived or died on the battlefield. I guess I was just lucky because I took chances no other Marine would think of taking. I was soon ruled unfit for combat duty. I was given the honor to tell Ben Abel's family about his death. This was one of the hardest things I have ever done.

Then government sent me to Japan for several months. When they thought I had recovered from my darlings death they sent me back to combat in Korea. What they didn't understand is that I would never recover from the loss of my beautiful and loving Molly she was my one and only love there would be no one else.

I was again sent back to Korea where while under heavy fire I was shot in the foot while trying to climb a large hill or should I say a mountain to get on the other side out of the line of fire. I couldn't walk but I could crawl, I crawled to the other side of the hill. I spent six months in the hospital over this injury my ankle has been weak every since.

It was nearing the end of my military career when eight of us Marines were given an order to accompany the body of one of our fallen comrades back home. I was the senior Marine we were not to let the body of our comrade out of our sight until it was in the ground. We got on the plane with the body and we got off the plane with the body we stayed with the body in the funeral home. It was hot and we had to be in full Marine dress. The Church was 20 miles out in the sticks where an automobile couldn't go. We carried the coffin 10 miles up hill another 10 miles on rough terrain but at least it was flat ground, which was a lot easier? We were not allowed to set the coffin down to rest or catch our breath. But thank-god the family helped us and shared in carrying the coffin. We took turns with eight of our comrade's family members. The family smelled like whiskey but was not inebriated to the point they couldn't help us. Of course it was against the rules for them to help us carry the coffin in any manner at any time. The problem was we just physically couldn't carry that coffin 20 miles without their help.

What we had not been told; is that his family worshiped the cottonmouth snake, or that they made there living by making and selling moonshine liquor. When we got to the Church, which was a small building there, were at least 80 people waiting for us, there were no children in the crowd. The Church was packed with human bodies there was barely enough room for us to walk though the crowd. We were instructed to set the coffin on a stand in the middle of the one room Church. The people squeezed together to make room for us to get through the crowd. The building had only one door, we were told to stand against the wall away from the door, out of everyone's way. Then someone opened a closet and pulled out a basket full of cottonmouth snakes and passed them around to everyone in the room except us. One of my comrade wanted to squeeze through the crowd and run. I told him to shut his mouth and stand at attention that he had to be still. As long as we didn't move the snakes would not hurt us, so he settled down after I told him that. We were all scared to death to move.

The people screamed and hollered and kissed their snake they wrapped these snakes around their bodies. They danced and sang and prayed to these snakes. These snakes had not been de fanged we could see the snake's fangs. Then some of the people started fighting. A very large woman that seemed to be the leader of these people hollered something and the people made a circle around her. She took off her shoes and socks and placed her bare foot on a very large snake's head. After several hours of this frightening ceremony they put the large cottonmouth snake; the one the large women had put her foot on and placed it in the coffin. Then we Marine Paul Bearers carried the coffin back into the small graveyard near the church where the grave was already dug. We stayed with our comrade until his grave was filled. Needless to say, we left as soon as possible. That is one experience we will all remember forever.

Again I was sent back to the mountainous area in Korea I had only seven months left to serve. Again we were under heavy fire the conditions were very poor. I watched my comrades go down like a person swatting flies most of them dead. Those that were not dead I couldn't get to because of the enemy fire I would've been killed trying to help them. I had no choice but to leave them behind. A grenade came from out of nowhere and exploded in my face. To this day I still wear the scars. When you look at me you think my face is terribly dirty, but it is from the grenade. I was sent to the hospital in San Diego where I stayed for two and a half years even though I just had about six months left to serve. They said, "We have you under observation" and they wouldn't let me go home. The doctors said I should have died but that I was too stubborn and spiteful to give up. I was lucky my eyes were not damaged the hospital staff talk about what a blessing this was. The Doctors picked bits and pieces of that grenade out of my face for many months. My parents believed God was looking after me and brought me back to them.

After a while I got bored while in the hospital so I asked if there was some kind of job I could do while I was there I was going nuts doing nothing. The hospital allowed me to work in the library, which I enjoyed very much. The library was peaceful I welcomed the serene atmosphere it presented. I no longer had to dodge enemy bullets. When I wasn't busy I was allowed to read all the books I wanted to. I used this time to further my education I read every book I had time to read. I like to read I also made a few very good friends that worked in the library too. The hospital wanted to operate on my ankle where I had been shot. I refused to allow them to operate I am not afraid to admit I am afraid of the knife. I said, "I will live with the pain no one is going to take a knife to me." It was bad enough having bits and piece's of that grenade dug out of my face.

I served for three years in Korea it was pure hell. The ground was made of rock it was very cold as hell in the wintertime but fairly comfortable in the summer. I was in a combat unit except when I was in the hospital. We couldn't eat our meals on time because of the enemy fire we learned to eat when we could. Some times it wasn't even one meal a day it was attempt to eat and you might die or go hungry and maybe you will live. I am one of the lucky ones to still be alive. I wake up in a heavy sweat at night because of my experiences in Korea.

I retired from the military with a 10% disability. I received $112. a month for my disability. It hardly seemed worth the pain I suffered there, especially the loss of my Molly. I kept myself occupied by reading a lot of books while I was in the hospital. Isn't it funny that the military works for one of the largest Country there is? But our country doesn't pay their people but minimum wage. They encourage the military people to apply for food stamps because of the low wages they receive. Military people are living on the poverty level.

My Captain and I became good friends; we learned to trust our very lives to each other. I am alive today because of the things he taught me. He visited me often while I was in the hospital infect he was the only visitor I had the whole time I was in the hospital. Even after I left the service, we stayed in touch with each other. We talked frequently about what was happening in our lives, we gave each other advice and even met a few times for coffee. He was the one person in my life that I could communicate freely with. We understood each other and helped each other when we could. I was indeed upset when he passed on. I can't count the times I laid my life in his hands and just obeyed his commands. He is a friend I have missed for a long time now. I learned a lot of hard lessons from him that saved my life many times. We were more than comrades we were like family I loved him like the brother I never had.

Finally the day came that I was released my parent's had moved to Garden City Kansas. They were afraid to fly, so they drove down by car to get me. I was glad to be out of the hospital the closer we got to home the more I had to face the fact that Molly wouldn't be waiting for me. She was gone fore ever and ever in this life. I would have to live without her. I became very depressed because I missed her so much. How could I go on with life without her? It took three days to drive home I was quiet most of the way my parents seem to understand they didn't break into my thoughts. It seemed they understood I was grieving at this time.

After spending eight years in the Marines and fighting a war, my friends couldn't understand why I couldn't get over Molly; only my parents seemed to understand. I saw a lot of pain and death in the service of our country that I had been able to handle. But, Molly was different I had not and could not face the fact that she was gone. I had to blame someone, so I blamed my country, using the excuse if I had been with her she would never have been in a car accident therefore I would not have lost her. I can't explain why I felt this way about her death.

I was bitter and hard to get along with for a long time. I had no ambition to do anything with my life. There was no reason for me to make a life for myself. All the reason I had to better myself ended with Molly's death. I could no longer fit in with my extended family members I couldn't make friends. I felt cheated out of life. Personal hygiene became a stranger to me after I left the service. It didn't bother me that I was dirty and looked unclean to others. Nothing mattered any more, I was alone except for my parents.

My family stuck their nose in the air at me; they sort of disowned me because I looked so much like a bum. They looked down on me and wanted nothing to do with me. The worst part was that I didn't care. Because of this I lost contact with my extended family, I have never cared to try to find them. I feel they are selfish and spoiled, as well as greedy people.

For my family to shun me at his time was defiantly not the best thing for them to do as far as my mental health went. I needed the love and support of my whole family not just my parents. But, it seem the extend family didn't understand this or maybe they just didn't care. I kind of became the black sheep of my family, at least I felt that way. I was the talk of the town for a while, some people felt sorry for me, I didn't want their pity. I needed their support and understanding. Other people just stayed completely away from me. Others would cross the street and walk on the other side of the sidewalk to keep me from speaking to them. I soon got so lonesome I wanted to die; I just was not brave enough to try and kill myself. No one could, would or even tried to bring me out of this state of mind except my parents. They were uneducated and getting old they didn't know what to say or how to go about helping me, but they tried. I appreciated their efforts and loved them for this. I finally came to my senses and tried to recuperate myself it was a hard and bitter time for me. The rest of the family made fun of me, even in public places when I dared to venture out. When I wasn't helping my father I stayed locked in my room. Sometimes I went to Mollies favorite spot by the lake and just sat there, or sat in front of the bank where she use to work pretending I was waiting for her.

I became the laughing stock of the people that was at one time my friends. People either stayed away from me or constantly put me down. Those I tried to renew my friendship with wanted nothing to do with me, they found any excuse they could to avoid talking to me. I felt like and outcast, but I didn't have the energy or desire to do anything about my situation. Life no longer had any meaning to me. All I had left was my memories. I began to live my life in a make believe world. I pretended that Mollie was sitting next to me, I had conversations with her. While I was daydreaming if anyone broke into my thoughts it made me angry, and I was rude to them. I lived this way for several months. People thought I was crazy. Maybe I was. Finally I snapped out of this kind of behavior.

CHAPTER THREE

I stopped my day dreaming and pretending but I didn't feel like working it was difficult for me to adjust from being shot at and to face the real world' to just being a normal citizen again. I had never had the time to morn for my beautiful Molly. While in my right mind. I realized I needed time to do this. I didn't even look for work for a year, instead I helped my father with his paper business without pay of course only because he insisted that I help him. He was trying to pull me out of my depression by trying to make me take an interest in something. I had saved money while in the Marines. I just needed some time for me and I took the time I needed to recuperate. I became a whole person again.

When I did get a job it was washing dishes there was nothing else available and it was time for me to get on with my life. I wasn't broke I had saved the money the government paid me after all I couldn't spend it until now. All the time I spent in the service. I was either in combat dodging enemy bullets or in a hospital. I had no chance to spend money, now I had no one but me to spend it on and I didn't feel like spending it on myself right now. Years went by I worked only enough to get by on to satisfy my parents they wanted me to save what money I had in the bank for later times. I guess they were afraid I would never pull out of this state of mind I was in.

My parents started pushing me to get interested in young ladies they wanted grandchildren. I dated a few young ladies that I knew; but it wasn't like being with Molly I couldn't get serious about any of them. It was just friendship I enjoyed their company I had fun with them and that is as far as it went; I was unable to get excited about any one of the young women. I dated. No one could take Molly's place in my heart I felt I just had to be true to her and I was. I think in my mind I just couldn't admit that she was gone.

I worked at washing dishes for a few months then another temporary job opened up paying more money and I quit washing dishes and started another job that I knew was just a temporary position. After that I was hired by a regional drug store chain and was doing very well. I took a lot of flack from my parents and other family members for not getting married and having a family over the next five years. I took so much flack that I dreaded to go around my family, they couldn't understand I was still carrying Molly around in my heart. I went through two managers and did just great. The third manager didn't like me and I didn't like him to say it nicely we didn't get along. I liked the owner of the store but he was never there.

Things came to a head when the new manager hired a new employee that was green and knew nothing about the business at $5 an hour more then I was getting paid, mind you I had been there five years. Then he had the audacity to tell me to train this new employee, this made me very angry. Through a friend of mine I learned that this new employee was a friend of the manager, this really pissed me off. I felt like I had been insulted. I was the one that should have received that $5 rises. My vacation was coming up the next week so I said nothing. The next week when I had my weekly check and my vacation check in my hand I took my vacation and never went back to work at the drug store. Later in the month I met the owner of the drug store on the street he asked me why I had never came back to work after my vacation. I told him everything he said, "I well investigate this." The next time I seen him he told me that he had fired the new employee and the manager. He then asked me to please come back and work for him again. "I said, "No I can't, your manager bit me in the ass, like a snake. All your employees know this. For me to come back would be the same as me sticking my butt out and saying kick me in the butt again. I would then look like a fool. I have to much respect for myself then that." I declined his offer.

About this time I met a young woman and almost married her, some how I just couldn't go through with it. We were from different worlds I still pined for Molly. It was not Judy's fault she was a proper young woman. It was I; I just didn't love Judy in the same way I had loved Molly. Also I didn't want to marry a woman just to make my parents happy. That wouldn't have been fair to her. We talked about marriage I told her how I felt. Her words was, "I wouldn't want to live in a dead woman's shadow; thank-you for being honest." We parted friends we are still friends today.

My dad, Geo Hooker

My father got sick my parents were getting up in age they were in there 60s, he was no longer able to work. I supported my parents for several years and helped my mother take care of my father. There were some things she was just not able to do alone. This time in my father's life was very hard for him he was used to being the breadwinner of our family. As well as giving a helping hand to anyone in need of his help. It was hard for my mother and I to see him in this state. He became very depressed and withdrawn he felt that he was less a man. We tried hard to help him deal with his situation but it was impossible. He had cancer and he knew it, we were unable to say or do anything to make him feel better. It was terribly hard for my mother to watch my father die. Father passed away in 1965. My mother died three days later from a heart attack. I believe she just couldn't face life without father, she grieved herself to death. It was very hard for me to lose both my parents so close together.

I was now alone in this world. I felt so alone I became very depressed and almost gave up myself. Again I knocked around doing mostly nothing. I worked only enough to sustain myself. I constantly thought about Molly and my parents. Again I dated a few women this did not help I still couldn't get close to any of them. I couldn't get intimate with a woman I guess It just didn't feel right to me. I think maybe I was afraid I would forget Molly. I never came to grips with the loss of Molly. I wallowed around in self-pity for a long time. For this reason I stayed celibate the rest of my life. There was no woman alive that could take Molly's place in my heart.

One morning I saw an ad in the paper saying, City Cabs, Cab Drivers wanted. This made me think of some of my experiences while traveling around the world. In Europe the cab driver set in the front seat there was no top over the driver: there was not even a door on the front of the automobile. The vehicle held only two passengers. This cabbie had picked up a huge male passenger. The passenger was so large he had got stuck in the back seat of the cab. I watch nine firemen trying to help this passenger out of the cab. They finally managed to get him out of that little car, but it took some time. The passenger was truly thank-full for their assistance and tipped each of them$20.

In Mexico there is a lot of traffic some of the streets are eight lanes wide while others were about the width of one of our allies. Sidewalks were twenty feet wide. If a cab driver was in a hurry he drove on the sidewalk to get around the traffic in front of him and then when he could he dr0ve back on the street. The first time the cab driver did this while I was riding in his cab it scared me to death. I wondered if the cabbie was crazy or just plain drunk.

One time I called a cab from a bar the driver got a second call to pick up another passenger it was a very well dressed elderly lady. The lady and I was sitting in the back seat the driver got a second call he stopped to pick up his third passenger. Now mind you this is a two-passenger cab. The third passenger would have to sit in the front seat with the driver. But this man was determined that he was going to sit on the elderly ladies lap. The driver asked the passenger what he thought he was trying to do and the man said I'm getting in your cab. The driver told the man to come around the car and get in the front seat. This male passenger was determined that he was going to set on the ladies lap. The elderly woman was getting quite upset. I doubled up my fist and knocked the man to the ground the cab driver sped away as quickly as possible leaving him lying in the street.

I thought of some of the experiences I had as a passenger in the different countries that I had traveled through, I chuckled to myself. I thought to myself it might be fun to drive a taxicab it would something different; I thought I would try driving a cab. I felt like I had nothing to lose so I set up an interview. The man that was recruiting cab drivers was Joe Gangi he was on the run from the mafia he had run off with some of their money and they wanted it back. I was trained and hired this was the beginning of a forty year job. I worked forty-nine days fifteen to sixteen hours a day without taking a day off. I began to get a grip on life again. I made money and pulled out of my depressed state of mind. Joe Gangi told me I could make $500 a day. I called him a liar, there were days I could and did make five hundred dollars a day after I learned the city but I couldn't make that every day. I had to work long hours to do as well as he said I would.

I soon learned I didn't know the city as well as I had to, in order to do my job right. I got myself a map and made learning the city a challenge I enjoy challenges When I didn't know where a street was I got out my trusty map, at night I had to turn on the headlights of the cab and stand in front of the cab, but I found the street I was looking for. I refused to call the dispatchers and ask for directions. Because I knew how to read a map and paid attention to the street signs even when I wasn't working I learned to be a good cab driver. I was never late picking up my passengers. Soon I had conquered the challenge of learning the city streets. I became a little restless, I need a change, and I was ready for an adventure. So off I went, I took what few belongings I had and moved to Chicago. That is one place I had never been.

I enjoy being a cab driver it is an easy and interesting job. I can pick my own hours to work. I don't have anyone looking over my shoulder. I have money in my pocket all the time. I like talking to my customers and listening to their life stories. I applied at Checker Cabs and was accepted as a driver. I believe this is where I learned a lot of patience.

I had many interesting experience as a cab driver I never got bored driving a cab. I did get disgusted many times.

While driving in Chicago, One evening a young woman jumped in front of my cab I either had to stop or run over her. She said, "Please I have no money, my son is bleeding from the nose, I can't stop the bleeding. Will you please take me to the closest emergency room? I will pay you I just can't do it now. She lived on the third floor I followed her into the alley and up the stairs. She had five small children I grabbed one under each arm we got the children in the car. By this time I was covered with blood. We put the children in the cab and I took off for Grant hospital.

When we arrived at the emergency room she had no one to stay with the other four children while she was in the emergency room with the child that had blood pouring from his nose. I stayed in the waiting room with the other four children so she could stay beside her son with the problem. He was maybe three years of age the child was frightened and he needed her at that moment. I sat three to four hours with the other four children before they decided to admit the little boy. As I drove her and the four children home she explained the problem her son had. I wasn't sure I understood everything she said I did understand some of it.

It turned out that the city had dispersed rat poison in the alleys trying to control the rats. The only way into her apartment was through the alley. The boy had absorbed the rat poison through the pores of his skin and was highly allergic to the poison. I saved a child's life that evening because the doctor said the child would have bled to death had his mother not sought help as quickly as she did. I was feeling pretty good about myself at this time. It didn't hurt me to help someone in need. I never expected to hear from this woman again. I guess some of the experience I had, hardened my heart a little.

One morning about a month later I went to work and the cashier said, "I have something for you a woman hand delivered it, he handed me an envelope. I opened the envelope I found a $100 bill and a thank-you note. The not said, "Thank-you so much I am sorry but, this is all I can afford." I was truly a surprised man! This didn't happen often. Sometimes it pays to lend a helping hand even to strangers.

Chicago was to big a city for me I didn't like it so I went back home to Wichita Kansas, and started driving a cab for Best Cabs Inc. I didn't have any trouble with my customers in Wichita but the other drivers were another story.

The other drivers liked stealing other drivers orders even the drivers from the same company would steal my order if they could beat me to it. I never had to lower myself to stealing someone's orders. I was able to make enough money where I did not feel the need to do this. Even on the bad days when there weren't many orders I refused to stoop to the level of stealing orders from other drivers. I considered myself better then that. When you are driving a cab you are virtually alone. If you have car trouble or run out of gas you will need another driver to come to your aid if the drivers don't like you they are not going to help you.

The dispatchers started a running joke about me. They placed a $20 bill in the file cabinet drawer. The dispatcher that could give me an order that couldn't find the address on won the twenty dollars. Fifteen years later the twenty dollars was still in the drawer. The dispatchers gave up and split the twenty between them. This became a company joke after that.

Customers like to have you get out and open and close the door for them. They like for you to load and unload their groceries for them. I always carry customer's groceries to their door. I never go inside their home. I always open and shut the car doors for them. Because I did this I usually got tipped more then the run of the other driver. Wheelchairs is a problem for me because of my injuries I received in Korea, but I manage to get them in my car and I have never lost one yet I always carry bungee cords to hold my trunk down. In those day's cabs was the main transportation. There was very little parking in Wichita so people took a cab to work, to the hospital, to home, or any place they needed to go. The city did have a bus service but it stunk. A person had to walk three miles or more to get to a bus and walk another mile or two to get to their destination. Only the very poor rode the City Bus'. As the years passed the city got jealous and each year they made rules and passed a city ordinance that the cab companies and cabbies had to follow or the City of Wichita would yank their license to operate away from them. This made it harder for a cabbie to make a living. For years the city made the rules for the cab companies they still do. The owners of the cab companies have less money then the drivers do plus a lot more headaches then most businesses.

A person seeking a job as a cab driver has to get a special license through the city, which cost money. A person looking for work usually doesn't have any money to pay for the inspection fees or the Cab license and wait three or more weeks for a job. So what happens is the cab companies are forced to take the people that no one else wants. There are still a few good cab drivers they drive a cab because they like to set their own hours.

It used to be that the city would run the check on a driver in an hour or two; not anymore now they take at least three weeks or more. A person with a hungry family can't spend ten to twenty dollars for the check the city does on them and the license; and then wait three or some weeks for a job. His family needs to eat now. So the decent people find a different kind of job before the city ever gives the cab companies permission to hire them. It is different when a person applies to drive a city bus the city will help a new bus driver get his CDL that they need to drive a city bus or school bus and put them right to work even though the city does the very same check on a bus driver that they do on a cab driver. In the old days the driver got his license the same day he applied for them it took maybe two hours.

The problem is the City Bus is in competition with the cab companies. Of course they want to make it hard for us. Cabbies and cab company owners feel this is not fair or right because of the competition between the businesses. Also there are now better roads; plenty of parking places, people bought their own cars. Each family has an average of three cars. All these things made it hard on cab drivers and made it where the only drivers a cab company can find is the low life of our society. At one time a cab driver was a respected man of the community. Now we are considered the scum of the earth; give us back our business and our pride so we can become human again. Drivers with families need to be able to support them. Here is something to think about. What would a city the size of Wichita do without a cab service in town? I believe a lot of people would suffer especially the elderly.

After a few years I became the third shift casher this allowed me to get to know a lot of the drivers. Some of the drivers owned their own cabs; there were a few fleet owners (a fleet owner is someone that owns more than one cab, which they lease out to other drivers.)

A Cabbie doesn't want to make a dispatcher angry even in the early days. A dispatcher can make or break you they have control of your pocket book. They get tired of the drivers that have to be lead into their order, a driver had better learn the city or he won't last long on the streets. They also get annoyed with the complainers this kind of driver makes a dispatcher crazy over something that doesn't amount to a hill of beans. It doesn't take them long to figure out who is serous about making money and who wants to sit on their butts and cry that they can't make any money. When I started driving a cab I was told I could make money only if I was willing to stay behind the wheel. If you are out of your cab all the time you can't hear the orders when they are dispatched to you that means you make no money.

I consider myself a good cab driver I have learned every inch of this city by heart. I develop a reputation of being a good cab driver this was very important. Because of my reputation the dispatchers knew they could depend on me. If they needed something done in hurry I got the fare this put more money in my pockets.

Once a cab ran out of gas on the air base with a passenger in the car, I was sent to help him. I bought a gallon of gas and took it to him as he was pouring the gas in his tank the passenger got into my cab and asked me to take her to her destination, which I did. The other cab driver complained to the company. They bawled me out; I asked them what was I suppose to do?

Was I supposed to manually pick her and her luggage up and toss her in the street? She came to my cab and got in on her own initiative. I didn't ask her to get in my cab. I had not even spoken to her. The manager of the company agreed there was nothing else I could do but take her to her destination. This made my fellow cabbie quite angry we were never friends after that.

There was one driver that called most of his orders in dead. (That means that he couldn't find his passenger on the other end.) I followed him around one night and picked up nine out of ten of the passengers he had called in as being dead. He was too lazy to get out of his car and knock on a door. Sometimes he wouldn't wait for a passenger to get down the stairs for him to be able to load them. He didn't take into consideration that an elderly person or a person with small children might take a little longer to go down a flight of stairs. Sometimes he just didn't like the way they looked. A cabbie can't make money with this kind of an attitude. This is the wrong attitude to have if you are driving a cab. As a cab driver you are a public servant you must act like it. The customer is never wrong in this business.

I picked up a woman at a club once, she was well dressed and wearing the highest high heel shoes I have ever seen. She handed me a hundred dollar bill and said, "I want to go to Wellington." While we were on our way to Wellington she said, "I might want to come back with you." After we got to Wellington she said, "Wait for 15 minutes and if I haven't come out you can leave." She came out and said, "I would like to stop in Park City for a minute." We stopped in Park City the man she went to see slapped her in the face so hard she fell to the ground. Let me tell you that little lady through she was small gave that man a whipping I don't think he will ever forget. She was one woman that could take care of herself.

Once I picked up a woman it was pouring down rain she said, "I have only five dollars take me as far as the five dollars will take me?" I asked her where she was going she gave me the address and said, "I know five dollars won't get me all the way home." I took her all the way home I just couldn't put the young woman out in the rain to walk the rest of the way home. About six weeks later I picked her up again. She pointed her finger at me and said, "I owe you some money." She paid me what she owed me and tipped me three dollars, I don't mind helping a person but I don't like being played for a sucker.

I always pick up a person that I felt was in need even if I know they can't pay me. Many times I have picked up women when I seen them running down the street with a man chasing after them and took them to a safe place most of the time without pay.

I meet all kinds of people and I learn something new from each one of them. This is part of the reason I stayed with driving a cab instead of getting a-nine-to five-job. I can work the hours I want to work. I can take time off when I need or want to. I just enjoy driving a cab.

I picked up a man from the airport wearing a five hundred dollar suit. I took him to his destination, when we got there he took out his wallet and started fanning through one hundred dollars bills, fifty dollar bills, when he got to the twenty dollar bills I grabbed a twenty that was what he owed me. I left I felt this man was rubbing his money in my nose I didn't appreciate it.

I picked up another man off the airport he had no luggage. He wanted to go way out in the county where there were no houses, maybe I could have found a cow if I had tried. He ordered me to take a gravel road, after we left the highway my mouth got dry. I began to think I might die. He starts loading a Mauser thirty shot machine pistol this made me nervous and frightened my mouth got dry. I didn't know whether he was going to shoot what or me. I'm not a brave man. I thought it was over for me at this time, I just knew I was a goner. When we got to the corner he said, "Stop I am getting out he threw five one hundred dollars bills over the seat and said, and "You did not see me." I quickly agreed that I had not seen him. He got out and I left and went back to town as quickly as possible without even looking back. I thanked my lucky stars I was still alive. I never heard any more about this passenger nor did I want to. I enjoyed the five hundred dollars though I often wondered if it was worth it. I felt guilty about not going to the police with this but I was afraid to do so. I believe he was a killer for hire but I really don't know. I was just glad to get him out of my cab. I have never told anyone about this until now.

I didn't read about any murders in the papers or hear anything about it on the news. I'm not sure if I would have told my story if I had. That's one thing about being a cab driver you want to be careful where you stick out your neck. Driving a cab is the most dangerous job in the world so the experts say.

About this time I stumbled on Aunt Dee she was old sickly and living alone she needed someone to look after her. She preferred to live alone. I did what I could to help her I helped her buy her medicines and helped her do her house and yard work. I saw to it that she had a nurse to take care of her personal needs every day. I learned to love her all over again she was my mother's favorites sister.

Aunt Dee had sons and daughters but none of them seemed to care about her enough to giver her the help she needed. I had no idea how to get in touch with any of them. My aunt had money which se refused to spend. I think she for got that she had any money. When I asked her for money to get her medicine she swore to me she was broke. If I did not get the medicine she did without it. So I paid for it out of my pocket.

When Aunt Dee passed on all her children showed up, there was quite an argument over her material passions. I didn't stick around to find out how much she was worth or who got what. I just did not want to be involved in such behavior. Besides it was none of my business. Not one of her children thanked me for taking care of their mother.

At this time I decided if this is what the extended family had turned out to be I did not want to be a part off it. Their behavior made me sick I walked away from the funeral vomiting and never looked back. That is the last I seen any member of the extended family. I don't feel like I'm missing anything after my parents, aunts and uncles passed away my extended family fell apart. I was ashamed to be related to them.

CHAPTER FOUR

I was given a fare to pick up at a bar one night, my customer a man jumped in the front seat which made me uncomfortable to begin with. He laid his head on my shoulder and his hands began to wonder in area's that was improper. I quickly stopped my cab and put him out. He was unhappy and called the company. I was mad at the customer so I said, "I am not a homosexual and will not put up with that kind of behavior." After explaining what had happen, the company agreed with me and said I was right to put the man out. This is only one of the dangers of driving a cab at night.

There was one particular school child that lived out in the country. The principal brought him out in handcuffs and placed him in the backseat of my cab then the principal removed the handcuffs. I sure wish he had left them on; I'm driving down the highway about fifty miles an hour when he opens the door and tries to get out. I caught him by the collar of his coat just in time to keep him from jumping. Obviously he didn't realize the danger or maybe he just didn't care.

I 'have transported a few school children that liked to standup and pee all over the back of the front seats they thought that was funny. I didn't feel the same way because I had to clean up their mess. Reporting such things to the parents or the school was a waste of my time. And of course you always get the drunks that vomit all over your cab. You might as well take the night off when that happens because your cab needs to be detailed after that.

To many times I have been sent to help a driver that run out of gas this always frustrates me. Things like this wouldn't happen if the driver would put more than two dollars worth of gas at a time in his car. Anyway this driver had passengers he grabbed the gas can from my hand and began putting it in his car. At that time the male passenger started walking toward my car with his wife following him he said, "I am late will you take me on to my destination." He and his wife got in the back seat of my car. By this time the other driver had put the gallon of gas I delivered to him in his car he came running back to my car yelling that I was high jacking his customer. He didn't offer to pay me for the gas or the can. I drove away and left the other cab driver ranting and raging. I asked the passenger how much the other driver's meter read he said, "ten dollars," I asked if it was alright with him if I stared his fare at ten dollars the passenger agreed to this. I figured the other cab driver and I was even. I feel it is stupidity for a cabbie to run out of gas in the first place if you put just a couple dollars at a time you lose money when you have to stop and put gas in your car so many times. At that time gas was nineteen to twenty-five cents a gallon. A cabbie could make a good living, which is not true today.

A few weeks later I was called to help the same driver he had a flat tire and did not have a jack. When the dispatcher told me whom I was to help, I lied and said, "I left my jack at home," of course the dispatcher knew better but he said nothing to me. He called another cab driver to help him instead. I was not a person to let myself be a sucker the second time.

I picked a woman at St. Francis Hospital she handed me a detailed map of where she wanted to go. The map was a piece of art it showed every stop sign, every light, every corner, and some of the main buildings like banks, hospital and hotels. I thought maybe she couldn't talk. I took her to her destination and said very loud because I didn't know if she could hear well, "It's nine fifty" the lady spoke up and said, "are you sure it was sixteen fifty when the cab took me to the doctor's office." I convinced her that the meter was right she gave me twenty-five dollars and said, "Thank-you for being honest keep the change."

The company rule was that driver was supposed to take care of each other. One morning I woke up and started to work when I approached my cab I had a flat tire. I didn't have a spare because I had given it to Jim Clark another driver the night before so I called the company to have some one bring me a tire. The company sent a driver named Johnny out to help me. Johnny charged me $15 for delivering the tire to me. Believe it or not I refused to help Johnny a few times. I thought about helping him once and making him pay me but decided against it because I didn't want to give myself a bad reputation. In this job your reputation means everything. If you had a bad reputation you had an awful hard time making it.

I have also helped many motorists that were not cabs without charge when the need was there. I even pushed a couple of women's car to their destination with my cab because they needed help and I couldn't get their car started they had no money to pay me and told me so before I pushed their car home for them. If someone needs help and don't have the money to pay me I can't just leave him or her stranded I wasn't raised that way.

One driver picked up a man with an electric wheelchair, He got the man in the cab and put the wheelchair in the trunk he didn't tie the trunk shut. He lost the wheelchair before he got to where the customer was going and didn't even know it. Of course when he got to his destination, which was a hospital the wheelchair was gone. Boy! Was this driver mad when he had to pay six hundred and fifty dollars for the wheelchair? But it was his fault for not tying the trunk down. The hospital let his customer borrow a wheelchair until his was replaced.

It would surprise the public to know how much crap a cab driver has to put up with trying to make a living. We pick up all kinds of people, angry people drunk people; people that are incontinent in your cab, old ladies, unsupervised children, and the police will even call us to pick up the drunks that they don't put in jail for what ever reason, most of the time they had no money to pay the fare with.

In the 40 years that I've driven a cab I have only had someone try to rob me three times. Once by a regular customer that I knew he was drunk, we were traveling north on I-35 highway when he put a gun to my temple and demand my money. I immediately stomped the gas peddle and as the saying goes I put the, peddle to the metal and started swerving deliberately. I said, "OK shoot me but I'm not going alone, you are going with me. Throw the gun out the window and we both will live." He throws the gun out the window. I kept driving north on I-35 until I was out of the city quite a ways I stopped my cab and told him to get out, I left him standing in the middle of no where. As I drove away I could hear him cursing me.

Another time I picked up a customer in a bad part of town, he didn't tell me his destination but, instead told me to go south on Hillside then he kept trying to make me turn down dead end streets, he pulled out a gun and held it to the back of my head. My hair stood up on the back of my neck but I still refused to turn I had a plan. I drove down Hillside until I came to Wesley Hospital then I opened the door and jumped out with the car still moving. I could see the customer scrambling over the front seat. I ran into Wesley Hospital's security guards office and they called the police. The company recovered their car on Lincoln and Hillside. The car was thank-fully in one piece. No one was arrested in this case.

I was dispatched to an adult club to pick up a passenger. It was summertime I'd been given a name to ask for. When I got to the club I ask, The bouncer who called for a cab?" The bouncer found the customer and brought him to me. The customer was in his mid forty's and about two thirds drunk. He gave me an address on the other side of town as his destination. After we left the club he told me to turn left toward town. About five blocks from the club he told me to turn right. I drove a block or so he told me to stop. He pulled a gun didn't try to rob me of my money but made me get out of the cab and took the cab. Three or four days later the Oklahoma City police called they had it in the pound yard. The car was stripped, the tires, motor and transmission was gone. All the equipment inside the car was gone. It was just a shell of a car. No one was arrested in this case either.

The cab company I worked for had gone through four owners and working on the fifth. Owner, a cab company is a lot of headache. Most people seem to think it's a piece of cake. It is not hard work but you must know how to handle people. If a company manger doesn't have knowledge of people they aren't going to be able to keep drivers very long. Or the drivers will steal you blind given a chance. A person has to know what they are doing to own a cab company.

There used to be a driver named David this was his second or third time he drove for Best Cabs he came and went all the time. If he got an order at a bar he wouldn't go inside he would sit out side and honk. This limited his income. Other drivers would have to go get his passenger we were friends but not good friends. He picked up a passenger at the bus station going to Hutchinson Kansas. On the way he passed a highway patrol car giving a ticket to someone else. The high way patrol motioned him to pull over he went on. The passenger paid $65-five dollars for his cab fare. The driver came back to Wichita on the same highway where the highway patrolman was waiting. The ticket he received for not stopping when the patrolman tried to flag him down was $85. The driver lost $20 for not obeying a patrol officer. Not to mention the price of the gasoline.

John was a dispatcher and he didn't like a driver named Bill. John was dispatching one Sunday afternoon second shift. John gave Bill a fake fare at 2500 North Market I was in the office at the time. At that time you could see out the window on the East side. We watched him drive up and down the street looking for the address. Bill had bragged he could find any order in town. We knew he couldn't find all his order's, this was our way of testing him. There was no such address we laughed at him as he drove back and forth. We finally told him the order had cancelled. Would you believe we were located at twenty-five thirty-three North Market we thought we were being funny. We didn't think about how much we embarrassed Bill.

Back in the days of oral dispatching you could here all kinds of stuff on the radio. I remember guiding the different drivers into their orders. About the same time it was still voice dispatching when an order was given to a driver going to the airport. They gave the order off an hour ahead of when it was due. It wasn't an easy street to find, it was not even on the map. I had a passenger in my cab I was on the other side of town from the airport order. When I unloaded my passenger I checked my map and discovered it wasn't there. I called the dispatcher and told him it was not on the map and if he could he better call and find out where it was they still had thirty minutes to find it. Dispatcher called Davis and didn't get an answer. He called me back and said I didn't get an answer do you have any idea where it is? I checked my map again and told him to go to Annie Street that it should be within two blocks of Annie Street. The driver-followed instructions loaded the passenger ten minutes late the passenger was outside in front of the house and didn't hear the phone. That is what comes of having street knowledge it makes it easier to find your way around. That driver couldn't find that address without a lead on approximately where to look.

A number of years ago I don't remember how long ago it was sometime ago though. The dispatcher gave me an order at Kellogg and Rock Road telling me to step inside and help with the luggage. As I did so among the luggage I saw a basket I recognized it was a snake basket. I had seen them before. The passenger was a very good-looking woman all dressed up. I said to the bellman, "You take this end of the basket and I'll take the other end." We picked up the basket and off we went to the trunk. The woman followed us and said, "Put it in the back seat." After a half of dozen suitcases were put in the trunk she got in the front seat. We went to the airport; somewhere along Kellogg Street at that time there was a cop car alongside of us in the other lane. About that time the snake decided to stick his head out of the basket, which was sitting behind the driver's seat I was the driver. The cop looked over at us and saw the snake. The snake was a python about twenty feet long. The snake's head was about the size of a football. The cop nearly lost control of the patrol car. At the next exit the cop left Kellogg Street we went to the airport. When the snake's head came out of the basket he was about a foot from me I was scared to death. I about wet my pants, was I ever glad to get that fare done with. The hundred and fifty dollars I got for this fare was not nearly enough for putting another ten years on my age.

One day a man took his pet skunk downtown, he ran into a friend of his and his friend invited him out to dinner and he couldn't take the skunk in the restaurant with them. The man decided to send the skunk home by cab. Guess who got the order after three other drivers refused to carry the skunk. I got the order I talked to the man he told me he wanted to send he skunk home alone. He told me it was deodorized and would ride quietly providing it was in the front seat. The dispatcher told me to let him know if I loaded which I did. Home was out in the country about twenty miles from where we were. He gave me $100 for the cab fare plus a $100 tip. The skunk was no problem the drivers who refused to carry the skunk made fun of me for many years over this skunk passenger. The total of $200 was worth eight days lease on my cab. I just let them laugh their heads off the last laugh was on me. I made a lot of money that week without putting in a lot of hours this skunk was worth my time.

One of the dispatcher asked me to pick up a friend of hers and take him to the airport. She was the company manger I thought she was a friend of mine. The fare was $35 but this man had no money. I began to wonder if she really was my friend after that. When I told her he didn't have any money she said, "I will take care of it." She never did pay me for that fare. I raised sand with her because she was the company manger, but the owner wouldn't do anything about it. He said, "That's between you and her I don't know anything about it." I felt I had been cheated by this dispatcher and was up set for a while. Realizing that these things happen sometimes, I got over it rather quickly.

In a situation like this many of the drivers would have held a grudge and refused to work with this dispatcher. I continued to work with her and continued to make money most of the time. I have not had life too bad. I have always gotten along and didn't need or want much, just a little company from time to time. I finally realized that other people have tragedies too. I wasn't the only one who lost my loved ones; this is when my healing began and this is when I quit feeling sorry for myself.

CHAPTER FIVE

One day a new driver was hired it was in the year 1975 I could see he knew what he was doing. After a while I began to wonder if he ever slept, it seemed he worked around the clock. He hadn't been there long when he bought his own cab. Soon after that he brought another cab and leased it out to another driver. This man kept building cabs until he had thirty cabs on the line. He was the largest fleet owner in town. His name was Joe he owned a building on north Broadway that had been a hand crafted sofa and chair business. He turned it into a garage to work on his cabs. At first he did all the mechanic work on his cars himself as time passed and he built his fleet of cabs he hired another mechanic.

It was common knowledge Joe's daughter had given her coat to another child because the child had come home from to school without a coat and it was very cold. When Joe's daughter got home without a coat and her mother found out what had taken place she went to the child's home to retrieve her daughter's coat. She found three children alone in the house the oldest being about eight years of age the youngest about three and a half and severely retarded. She learned from the oldest child that his father drove one of Joe's cabs. Believing this driver was having a hard time financially; Joe's wife took the children home with her and called the cabstand to let the children's father know where his children were. The driver's name was Harry when he came to pick up his children that night she learned there was no mother in the picture, and the driver had been leaving the children alone while he drove to earn enough to care for his children so the driver told Joe's wife Frankie. She volunteered to care for the children free of charge while their father worked. Harry bragged to the other drivers that Joe's wife was his babysitter for him and how it came about that she was doing this for him. Harry said, "She is an old softy I bet $500 I can get in her pants." Some of the other drivers told warned Harry to leave Joe's wife alone.

One morning Joe called Harry into the garage. Joe was very angry. I remember thinking boy! Am I glad I'm not the driver he is angry with? I had to stick around the garage be cause my car was being worked on I couldn't help seeing and hearing what was going on. Joe stuffed three thousand dollars in Harry's mouth and fired him. Joe said, "Did you think my wife wouldn't tell me about this?" After yelling at him for thirty minutes and believe me Joe could yell louder then any other person I have ever heard he fired him. It sounded like when Harry the driver came to get his children from Joe's wife. Harry offered Frankie three thousand dollars to go to bed with him the he evening before.

Joe owned a large German shepherd dog that was very protective of his wife. This dog liked to stay in the corner of their bedroom. Frankie knew the dog was there so she said, "Okay but give me the money first." Harry gave her the money; she went into the bedroom and lay down on the bed. Harry followed her into the bedroom and lay down on the bed. At this point Frankie jumped out the other side of the bed. Then Harry started to complain in a loud voice. Joe's wife said, "You asked me to go to bed with you, you didn't say anything about having sex with you. You didn't say I had to stay in bed." By this time the dog was standing in front of Joe's wife with teeth bared Frankie grabbed the dog and told the driver to get his kids and leaves. Harry took a step toward her and she allowed the dog to lunge forward just a little. Then she said, "Leave or I will turn him loose. Then Harry left taking his children with him cursing loudly as he left Joe's home as Joe's wife stood by holding her dog. When Joe came home that night his wife told him what had happened and gave Joe the three thousand dollars. Joe told his wife, "I will take care of this which he did.

Later I overheard this story as Joe told it to his mechanic after he fired Harry whom I had witnessed and now understood Joe's state of mind. Now mind you I'm just a bystander over hearing a conversation I should not have heard. As an on looker I learned Joe could get very angry when it was necessary and I decided that I never wanted to be on the other end of his wrath.

This driver had the nerve to start driving for Russ and was later found dead in his cab. He was from New Orleans and had ripped off a casino there. We all believed that someone from New Orleans had caught up with him. What happened to his children I don't know?

This is an example of how rotten some people can be. Not all drivers are rotten but neither are all drivers good. We are people there is good and bad people in all jobs.

Joe often bought his two young sons to the garage with him when there was no school. The older boy was the kind of child that couldn't stay out of mischief. This boy actually set a fire in the middle of their garage floor.

That boy could be a royal pain in the ass at times. He appeared to be a very stubborn and lazy child. On the other hand the younger child wanted to help his father fix the cabs. This child was maybe four years of age. He soon learned the names of the different tools and became a good helper to his father. Joe no longer had to crawl out from under a car to get the tools he needed. He told the child what he needed and the young boy would hand his father the tool. As the younger child got older he worked side by side with his father after school and on the weekends during the summer he was beside his father all summer. I remember one Saturday I walked into the garage the boy was about seven years of age. Joe had a car on the front-end lift. Some how Joe hand managed to get his arm stuck under the car and couldn't get it out. In the process of trying to get his arm unstuck Joe hand managed to shift the car into neutral from underneath the car. I walked through the door as the car started to roll off the front-end machine. I saw this child run in front of the car and try to keep the car from rolling running over his father. As soon as I understood what had happened I ran over and help the boy hold the car. I managed to get in the position where I could shift the car into park. Between the two of us we finally managed to get Joe's arm unstuck. If I hadn't walked when I did the car would have run the child over and tore Joe's arm off. Had I been a little slow in assessing the situation the boy would have died trying to save his father? Joe would have been missing an arm. Now this is what I call real love for a parent.

The older boy was in the front of the shop digging change out off the creases in some extra car seats setting in the front of the garage unaware of his father's predicament.

The difference between the two boys fascinated me. I enjoyed watching father and son work together. Then I learned that the older boy was really Joe's grandson that he had adopted. I would have never have guessed from the way he treated the boys. The smaller boy was proud to go to the shop with his father; it bored the older boy because he wasn't interested in mechanical work of any kind. Maybe I should say work of any kind.

Joe was a good mechanic but defiantly knew nothing about keeping books him and his mechanic had receipts everywhere even on the floor. After awhile Joe hired a second mechanic he wasn't too good he drank all the time. I soon learn that Phil was his stepson and Joe had given him a job only because he didn't want his grandchildren going hungry. So he made a job for his stepson. This didn't work out but it wasn't Joe's fault it didn't work.

Joe kept his cars up better then any of the other fleet owners, drivers fought to be able to drive one of Joe's cars. When his stepson worked on a car he only did a half job. This caused problems between Joe and Phil. Phil constantly abused his mother.

The second largest fleet owner was Russ he had seventeen cabs on the line. The differences between Joe and Russ were Joe kept his cars running well. Russ just fixed everything he could with bailing wire. When he had to get a part for a cab he got used parts. His cars were not any good and he couldn't keep drivers for that reason. Everyone wanted to drive Joe's cabs. We stood in line waiting for Joe to add another cab to his fleet.

One of Russ' drivers took a car out it lasted forty-five minutes. The driver came back and got the second car, the cabbie drove that car ten miles and he had trouble keeping it running. So the driver called the dispatcher to have the third car towed in. After all that the driver return to the cab company and said to Russ, "I will never driver one of your stinking cars again.

He approached Joe and asked if Joe had a car for him. Joe had to buy another car he fix it up for him to drive, and that is what Joe did. It took him a couple of days to get the necessary equipment installed in the cab and have it painted. The driver was elated.

IRS audited Joe that year; Joe had no idea what to do. He brought his wife to the garage to try and fix the problems she by trade was a nurse. Frankie Joe's wife started trying to gather up all the receipts she could find. Of course it was impossible to find all of the receipts. Joe just dumped this problem in her lap and told her to fix it. This was what is called shoebox accounting she did the best she could. She accounted for all but three thousand dollars, which they had to pay the IRS. In the mean time her son Phil gave her an awful bad time.

Phil would shout at his mother and tell her she had no business being there to go home. He cursed at her, shoved her around and even threatened to hit her with his fist. I learned later that her name was Frankie I knew there was something familiar about her but I couldn't place her in my mind. She carried a small newborn Africa American baby with her to work. I learned later this was her grandchild. This child was the most beautiful child I had ever seen.

The fourth owner of the company was an elderly woman and wanted to sell the cab company and retire. She was making plans to join her daughters in Arizona. Her name was Sue her husband ran around the company pretending to be a big shot aggravating everyone. His wife did the work at the company all of us knew that. But he did do a good job of irritating the drivers we mostly tried to ignore him. Sue's husband had a stroke and died about two months later. It was then the latter part of 1990. This was very hard on Sue she looked drained all the time.

I have an elderly aunt still alive and I have bought her medicines for her, and help care for her she is the only family I have left. She had plenty of money she just didn't spend it. She would do without her medicine before she would buy it, to get her to take her medicine I by it for her. I too had been ill with pneumonia. Since I was a lease driver instead of a shift driver I had to pay the cab company whether I worked or not. I got behind on my lease payments to the tune of several thousand dollars. I wasn't trying to take advantage of Sue or anything like that I was just too sick to work long hours at a time. My aunt was too cheap to help me.

When Sue started talking about selling the company many drivers just stopped paying their lease. Sue either didn't care or was so occupied with trying to get her things in order so she could sell the company as fast as possible, she didn't realize what was going on around her.

Many of the drivers including me owned the company a lot of money. Some of the driver's owed as much as eight thousand dollars one of them owed fifteen thousand. Almost every driver in the company owed a lot of money and bad mouthed the old lady to boot. You can rest assured I wasn't in on the bad mouthing. I owed her money only because my aunt took a turn for the worst and I myself had been sick. I was doing the best that I could at the time.

I think what got me the most, was the drivers took advantage of this elderly lady that owned the company. She was up in her eighty's at least. At the same time they were talking and saying bad things about her on the streets. A few of them even called her a bitch; I just couldn't take part in this. I made quite a few enemies because I told them I didn't want to hear that kind of garbage. That the old woman had one of the biggest hearts I had ever seen in my life.

The old lady that owned the company had been so busy trying to take car of her husband that was ill and the business for several years that she was just worn out. Now that her husband was gone she seems to be very distracted and tired. She was looking forward to joining her daughter in Arizona. She planned to open a flower shop there.

She had several people interested in the company one was Joe. He had the largest fleet of cabs on the line and felt he needed to protect his investment. If someone else bought the company he may be forced to take his fleet of cabs off the line. He couldn't take the chance that someone else would buy this company out from under him and make him take his fleet of cars off the line.

Sue understood this and knew Joe had a good head on his shoulders. Unlike some of the other prospective buyers she believes Joe would run the company fairly. Sue agreed to sell the company to Joe and his wife in the early part of 1991. She had plenty of bidders besides Joe and could have gotten more money out of the company had she sold it to someone else less competent.

Sue liked Joe and his family so she chose to sell the company to them. This made a few people unhappy from the get goes to say the least because Sue had taken the lowest bid they felt cheated. This especially made Russ mad the second largest fleet owner. He had been with the company the longest and believed he should've had the company.

Russ talked to the office girls and told them to make it as hard as they could for Joe's wife to learn the business they attempted to make it impossible. When she walked in the front office the girls working in the office told her to get out of the office

Frankie left without complaint. As time went on she refused to do stay out of the office, one morning she said, "I will soon own this company and you are going to teach me what I need to know to operate it sufficiently whither you like it or not." Sue stepped in and told them Frankie was right. Many of the people associated with the cab company hated Frankie at this time. I believing they were learning they could not put anything over on her.

The girls put up the pretence of teaching her, but they deliberately left out some of the dollar figures that were necessary to make the books balance. Or they added dollar figures, which made the task of balancing the books impossible. Then they made fun of her because she couldn't get the books to balance. It took Frankie a while to figure out what they were doing.

They did not want Frankie to know what was going on in the front office, because they were stealing from the company and were afraid they wouldn't be able to cover their tracks enough to keep her from finding out if she learned how to do the book keeping.

She out smarted those two girls and took an accounting course at the Vocational Tech School in the evening while Joe watched the baby. It was hard to get anything over on this woman. She was as stubborn as a person could get so I thought.

When she set her mind on doing something she found a way to do it, even though she might have to kick a few innocent shins to accomplish her goal. She would apologize when she learned a person was innocent. I butt heads with her a few times and so did many of the other drivers. We had to learn her ways she is different then most people. If she didn't understand, you Had to keep talking until she did. She was a good listener as long as you didn't insult her. She tried her best to be fair to all of the drivers. Sometimes she bent over backwards to far trying to help or understand a driver, dispatcher, order taker or office worker.

She had no worldly wisdom and was as incent as a child on many things I felt like most of the time she was a breath of fresh air, but she had her why of getting under your skin, when she was trying to learn something or figure out something that didn't seem right to her. Her ignorance gave us lots of headaches, but also gave us many laughs. I have not said this woman is dumb; that is far from the truth. She just sees or understands all the evil that goes on in the world or around her, for that matter. She looks for the best in everyone. Dirty jokes she does not understand.

The drivers in the company educated her some but she is still very naïve today. I believe the fault in heart, she has an exceptionally good heart. She told me once that this world was not good enough for people to live in. Looking at her point of view

She made me feel better a bout not bringing children into this world. Seeing things through her eyes, I can understand what she meant, although I am still very lonely.

CHAPTER SIX

Joe and his wife Frankie became the fifth owner of Best Cab Company. Frankie begins taking the lease money at their garage because she had to bring her granddaughter with her. When this child got to be one year to fifteen months of age, when the drivers came in to pay their lease, this little girl held her hands out and the drivers gave her pennies. I was told the child had collected more then four hundred dollars in pennies by the age of three. Her grandmother took the pennies and bought her the Hooked on Phonics Program. It was amazing to walk into the office and see a child this young reading books. This child at the age of four was reading like a second grader. I enjoyed this child.

Frankie felt that she should begin learning the business slowly. She looked into the books and found the drivers owed the company a lot of money; her solution to that was the driver would pay at least $10 dollar a day more then their normal lease fee to get caught up. Most of the drivers had a fit they felt she didn't have the right to make them pay any thing they owed previous to when her and her husband had bought the company. Some of the drivers quit instead of paying what they owed. Slowly the drives that stayed with the company got caught up on what they owed. All but me my elderly aunt took up a lot of my time and I was getting up in age myself my health was failing me as well. I just wasn't able to do what I use to do.

I knew I had met this woman before; I just could remember where. Most of the drivers called her the Wicked Witch of Wichita, and many of them a lot worse things. I came close to slapping her a few times my self. But I knew she was green and knew nothing about the Cab business. I also knew that she was trying to learn and was trying to learn and had walked into a mess. She really rode the drivers to get caught up on their leases, which made every one mad including me. Some of the drivers gave her the same old sob story over and over a gain. One of the drivers told her he couldn't pay his lease because his mother had died; the problem was that he had told her that 8 times before. She was a smart woman she ask him, "What is your mother a cat? If so she has only one life left, you had better tell her to be careful!" I got a kick out of that.

She always took the time to search a drivers work history. She knew how many hours he had worked, and approximately how many orders he had taken. It was hard for a driver to put anything over on her period.

In her research she found that the office girls were embezzling for the company. One of the girls took money from the cash register and made charge tickets for the amount she took out, and counted the charge tickets as money at money at the end of the month when the books were closed. It didn't take the new owners long to catch on to what they were doing. Of course she was fired. Then the girl tried to collect unemployment.

Well the owners weren't going to have that. They gathered all of the paper work and went down to the unemployment office, and showed them why the girl was fired; they didn't have to pay the woman anything.

It was my turn to talk to the owners, I was called into the office to see Frankie; she had looked into my records and found that I hadn't been working very many hours a day. She pointed out that I owed the company a lot of money and couldn't pay it back working such few hours. She asks me, "Why are you not working more hours?" I said," I have an elderly aunt that I have to take care of. I buy her medicine that she has to have most of the time. I'm not feeling so good myself and am doing the best I can." She forgave my debt and let me continue to work. I thanked her from the bottom of my heart and tried to do better. I know of several other drivers she did the same thing with. The difference was I appreciated what she had done for me. The other drivers continued to bad mouth her behind her back, which I found hard to swallow, But I realized I had done the same thing until she recognized that I truly had a problem and extended a helping hand to me. I don't know how many drivers she helped. I do know it was quite a few, and most of them took advantage of her kindness. She was forced to become a lot tougher on the drivers, in order to keep the business going. It is hard to help some one who doesn't want to help him or her self. I had never seen a cab company, or any other company for that matter take so much interest in their employee's and contractors as this company was now doing. I felt, "Wow this is great!

It was about this time I was able to remember where I had seen this woman. She was the woman that I had taken to the emergency room with the child hemorrhaging fro the nose in Chicago. I thought that it was quite ironic that 30 years later our paths would cross again or this woman and her husband had bought the cab company and became my boss.

The boy that mistreated her so badly was the child whose live I saved that evening. She has been good to me through the years since she has owned the company.

Sherry another office girl who took care of the cashiering, was caught taking $40 from the drivers and sticking it in her pockets, and marking the driver off as vacation time he didn't have coming, or marking him as paid through the week. The lease on a car was $450 a week at the time. The cab company just wasn't making the money it should have been making. When the owners checked into why, they found the cashier was stealing money and allowing the drivers to steal money from the company as will, this girl was fired also.

Many of the drivers gave them a bad time because as I said she was green and just trying to learn the business, but she was always fair and honest. She has an uncanny way of speaking her mind exactly like she thinks it. Until you get to know her it is easy to get your feelings hurt when speaking with her. Once you get to know her you understand she is a person that just can't beat around the bush she has to say what's on her mind. And a lot of the time with very little if any tact she also expects you to do the same. If you have a bone to pick with her she expects you to speak up and tell her about it. She calls a driver in and talks to him when she receives a complaint on him. She also tells a driver when someone complements them and gives them a pat on the back.

One driver had a five-year-old son that had diabetes and nearly died, he owed a large amount of money to the company the company forgave his debt, and loaned him a car so he could get his child to the hospital. It made quite a few other drivers mad when the company allowed this driver to take a vacation in the car they had loaned him. This driver was so appreciative of the help they received, that when things got tough and the owners were having personal problems of their own. He quit and went to work for the competition during the time the company owners were trying to deal with four deaths in the family.

Some of the drivers started giving Frankie a hard time saying, "it is impossible for you to run a cab company when you do not even have a cab license, and can't even drive your cabs." She studied the driver's manual for a week and went down to city to take the test. Many drivers placed bets that she would fail the test she aced the test and made the drivers eat their words. She came out $150 a head after that the saying got started, "Don't mess with this woman; she'll bet you every time.

One thing I still laugh about today is the time their 16 year daughter told them a cab driver that was driving one of their cabs: tried to force her in his cab while he was saying inappropriate things to her, Their daughter told her parents about the incident giving them the cab number, The next morning when the girl's mother went to the shop she waited for the driver to come in to pay his lease. She only had the cab number to go with, so when the cab pulled into the garage and the driver got out of the cab she ordered him to come in and speak to her. She said, "Drop your drawers and get on your knees, lay it right here." She pointed to the front-end machine. Then she pulled a bayonet of its sheath and said, "I am going to teach you not to try and pick-up teen-age girls for sexual reasons." I knew she wasn't going to use the bayonet but was just trying to make a point.

The driver stuttered and stammered and said, "What are you talking about? I have not tried to pick up any young girls." Frankie said, "That was my daughter you tried to pick up over at Friends university." The driver stood in front in front of her shaking like a leaf and tried to explain that he was gay and had no interested in little girls. Her answer was, "My daughter said cab number 61 tried to pick me up and even nudge me toward the cab last Friday and, mind you, that its one of our cabs you are driving." Poor old Bill explained to her he had just picked this cab Sunday morning because his cab had broke down. She had to verify this with the front office before she put the bayonet back in its sheath. She apologized to Bill for making this mistake. Bill accepted her apology, but couldn't keep his mouth shut. The story was soon spread throughout the company and soon became a big company joke, only it was told in a vulgar way.

I stepped outside and rolled in laughter. Because Bill was gay and the expression on Bill's face was the funniest thing I think I'd ever had seen in the company. These new owners did a lot of funny little things like this to demonstrate their point, I guess because they were used to dealing with her children, and she treated the drivers a lot like they were her children.

The driver who had tried to pick up her daughter got word of what she had done and quit before she had a chance to speak to him.

As it turned out Frankie and Bill the driver she mistakenly accused of picking up her daughter, became good friends a few years down the road. In fact, they had lunch together two days before he was found dead in his apartment. He had told her he was afraid for his life at that time, but didn't say why.

Frankie often took a driver to lunch if he wanted to talk about something he didn't want the whole cab company to know about. She was good about keeping a driver's confidence On the other hand, if she had a bone to pick with you, she was not bashful about setting you straight. In time the good drivers learn to respect her. She calls this going out and throwing knifes, forks, and spoons at each other until they became friends. And to everyone's amazement, the driver that had gone to lunch with her always came out of the restaurant with a newfound respect and friendship with her. Her husband used the pool hall in the same way.

Finally the day came that our new owners gained control of their business. Today we have computers in our cabs. We are the only company in this city that does. It is saver to drive for Best Cabs because the dispatcher can now tell where each and every cab is at all times, which street it is on, what direction it is going and how fast it is going. If a customer gives a driver trouble all the driver has to do is say our secret word and the dispatcher sends the police to help them.

Once Frankie was on her way to work driving down I 35-the police had the exit she needed to get off at was block off with police cars. She is a person who can get lost going around the block. Believe it or not, she got lost and couldn't find her way to the company. She called the dispatcher and told him she was lost. The dispatcher ask her where she was, she said, "Hell, if I knew where I was I would be lost, now would I? All I can tell you is I am surrounded by fields. There are fields everywhere and no street signs. I am just lost that's all"?

The dispatcher sent me to find her it took me a while; all I knew that is that she was going north on I 35 because she lived on the South side of town. I did find her, but it took me a while. This was quite a joke around the cab company for quite a while. She had a hard time living that one down. When a driver got lost the dispatchers would yell loud enough for her to hear, "Send our boss, then he can wind up in Kalamazoo Michigan, and we won't have to put up with them any more." She was teased a lot about this but she was able to laugh the comments away. I still think this is funny I still laugh about this sometimes.

Finally the day came, when the company had to tell me I was an accident waiting to happen and took my cab from me this left me homeless. I could no longer make a living for myself. This couple learned I was sleeping on a park bench, and hunted me down to give me a place to live. They have helped me get my finances straightened out to where I can live fairly comfortable. I am no longer hungry. They see to it that I get to the store and the laundry when I need to go. I am enjoying my retirement at his time: my only problem is transportation.

I was surprised and happy to realize, that there was still people who lived by the old fashion code of life. Someone that still recognized the fact that we all originated from Adam and Eve and in essence we are all brothers and sisters. The human family has the obligation to be each other's keeper when the need is there. The bible says let the lazy man go hungry, but there is a difference in being lazy, to sickly, to old or being a child unable to provide for your own needs. There is an old saying (what goes around comes around). I believe that this is true, at least for me it is. I have always help people when I could. I tried to be kind and considerate to people. Now it is my turn I need help and I am receiving it for which I am very thankful. Never dismiss the old wives tales and remember what goes around comes around. Keep in mind you too will be in need of help some day. Will you receive it? That depends on what you are doing now.

I will take all the fond memories of my working years and my childhood to my grave. They will keep me occupied as I laugh about all the funny and odd things that have happened in my lifetime. I am proud to have been a part of this company. I wrote chapters five and six because my story wouldn't be complete without explaining how I became part of the cab company's family so I shared these precious memories with you as well. My friends tell me I am part of their big family the Best Cab Inc family. I share the hard times and the good times with my new founded family. Don't tell me it doesn't pay to help someone. This couple has paid me for the help I gave this woman one hundred fold. I have lived a long and happy life my only regret in my life; is that I lived it without my Molly.

EPILOGUE

I told my story partially to give me something to do for a while and also hoping it would help relieve some of the pain, I still feel over the lose of my Molly.

I had a wonderful childhood, and what I thought was perfect parents. I never knew the meaning of hunger during my growing up years. My family always had plenty of food, for us, and also our neighbors when they were in need. I felt loved by my immediate family and my extended family. We didn't have money but we always had food, we raised a big garden with everything imaginable in it. We worked together and we worked hard.

I fell in love with a beautiful girl during my senior year of high school. After graduation I went into the Marines, with plans to marry Molly when I returned. While I was in the service Molly died in a car accident I never got over this. I have remained unmarried waiting to join Molly.

After the service I had no desires except to pine for Molly. I didn't want to work, I had no interest in anything except wallowing in my self-pity. The extended family gave up on me. I guess I sank about as low as a man can sink, as the old saying goes I hit rock bottom, and stayed there for a few years. My parents were the only ones that tried to help me out of this state of mind. They didn't know how to go about trying to help me, but they tried. I love them for this.

Finally I began to pull myself up by the bootstraps, it took me a long time. I had gotten myself a good job and was doing fine when my father got sick with cancer.

I worked and supported my parents during this time. Father passed away, mother died three days later with a broken heart. This sent me right back down into the slumps. I lost track of the extended family. The worst part is that I didn't care. Again I was content wallowing around in my self-pity. I was alone I was truly alone this time, that is all that went through my mind. Again I had to reach rock bottom before I could pull myself up by the bootstraps. No I didn't drink I never did do that. I just had no will to survive. I couldn't work, I didn't want to eat. I didn't want to do anything but relieve my past life in my mind. I wanted to pretend that I still had Molly and my parents.

The day came when I realized that I had to work or die. I seen an ad in the paper : CAB DRIVERS WANTED. I became a cab driver and loved it. I drove a cab for forty years. The day came when I was too old to drive. The owners of the cab company were forced to retire me. In other words they took my cab because I was an accident waiting to happen. Because I had no family and nowhere to go this family sort off adopted me, and I adopted them. Except for not being able to drive when I want to go somewhere I am happy.

Once more I have a large family.